The
SMALL and MIGHTY
Book of
Space

Published in 2022 by OH!
An imprint of Welbeck Children's Limited, part of Welbeck Publishing Group.
Based in London and Sydney.

www.welbeckpublishing.com

Writer: Dr Mike Goldsmith, Fellow of the Royal Astronomical Society
Illustrator: Kirsti Davidson
Design and text by Raspberry Books Ltd
Editorial Manager: Joff Brown
Design Manager: Matt Drew
Production: Melanie Robertson

ISBN 978 1 83935 149 5

Printed in Heshan, China

10 9 8 7 6 5 4 3 2 1

The
SMALL and MIGHTY
Book of
Space

Dr Mike Goldsmith and Kirsti Davidson

Contents

Star-Gazing
9

Solar System
31

Stars
67

Space Travel
89

The Universe
and its Galaxies
125

INTRODUCTION

This little book is full of planets,
moons, and more stars than
you can shake a stick at.

All these things lurk high
above the air of planet Earth,
drifting and spinning through space.
Discover how we can explore
them with telescopes,
rockets and robots too.

USA

And find out about . . .

🪐 a space-ghost and space-ghouls

🪐 trees from the Moon

🪐 Santa in space

🪐 why astronauts don't burp

. . . **and lots more.**

Turn the page, and meet the Universe!

Star-Gazing

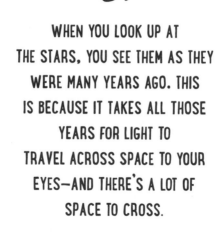

WHEN YOU LOOK UP AT
THE STARS, YOU SEE THEM AS THEY
WERE MANY YEARS AGO. THIS
IS BECAUSE IT TAKES ALL THOSE
YEARS FOR LIGHT TO
TRAVEL ACROSS SPACE TO YOUR
EYES—AND THERE'S A LOT OF
SPACE TO CROSS.

People who study **STARS** are called astronomers, because **"ASTRUM"** is Latin for star.

ASTRONOMERS MEASURE **DISTANCES** IN SPACE BY THE TIME IT TAKES LIGHT TO CROSS THEM. ONE **LIGHT YEAR** IS VERY ROUGHLY **6 TRILLION MI.**

THE SUN

is a STAR. It only
looks so much brighter
than other stars because
it's so much closer than
the rest (you should
never look at
it directly).

SUNLIGHT

is made deep inside the Sun, and then takes more than 100,000 years to make its way to the surface. Then sunlight moves very fast indeed, reaching the Earth just 8 minutes later.

In space, light is the FASTEST thing there is.

THE SUN

SHINES ON THE EARTH ALL THE TIME, LIGHTING ONE HALF OF IT. IT IS **DAY** ON THAT HALF AND **NIGHT** ON THE OTHER. THE **EARTH** TURNS, CARRYING YOU AROUND WITH IT.

IT TAKES **24 HOURS** TO GO AROUND ONCE. THIS IS ONE NIGHT AND ONE DAY.

IT TAKES **ONE YEAR** FOR THE EARTH TO GO AROUND THE SUN.

14

THE SKY

is blue during the day because blue light from the Sun spreads all over it. The sky is so bright we can't see the stars during the day, but we can sometimes see the Moon.

When there's not much
LIGHT,
like at night, humans
can't see colors—which is
why the **STARS** look **WHITE.**
In fact they are different
colors from deep **RED**
to **BLUE**-white.

The

STARS

become visible after SUNSET, if
it's not cloudy. You see different stars
at different times of NIGHT, different
times of YEAR, and from different
places on EARTH.

Centuries ago,
ancient people started
to name the patterns
of stars in the sky
(called **constellations**).
Most are people—like

ORION THE HUNTER
—or animals—like

TAURUS THE BULL.
But there is also
a clock, a chisel, and
an air-pump up there.

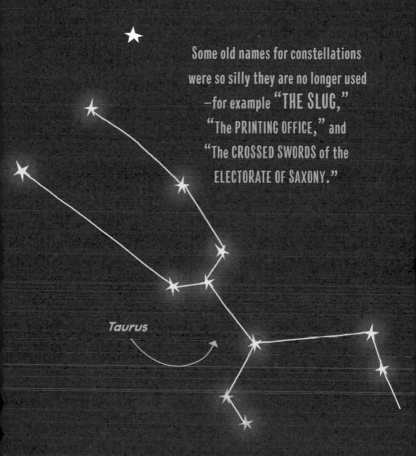

Some old names for constellations were so silly they are no longer used —for example "THE SLUG," "The PRINTING OFFICE," and "The CROSSED SWORDS of the ELECTORATE OF SAXONY."

Taurus

19

One of the easiest
constellations to find is

ORION THE HUNTER

—look for the three
stars in his belt.

Orion's belt

SHOOTING STARS
(also called METEORS) aren't
really stars—they are bits
of dust falling through the
air from space. They get very
hot and burn up, causing
STREAKS OF LIGHT in the sky.

The brightest starlike thing in the sky
is a planet: our space neighbor

VENUS.

It stays near the Sun, so it can
only be seen at the start
or end of the night.

Venus

Apps and websites tell
you how to find the
planets in the night sky,
as you can't see
all of them every night.
The easiest to see are
VENUS, JUPITER, MARS,
and SATURN.

NEBULAS

are cloudy patches in the sky, and there are many kinds. Some are named after what they look like—like the CAT'S EYE, the Horsehead, the Little Ghost, and the WITCH'S HEAD.

The scariest nebula is the

HOURGLASS

—which should really be called the Giant Scary Eye nebula.

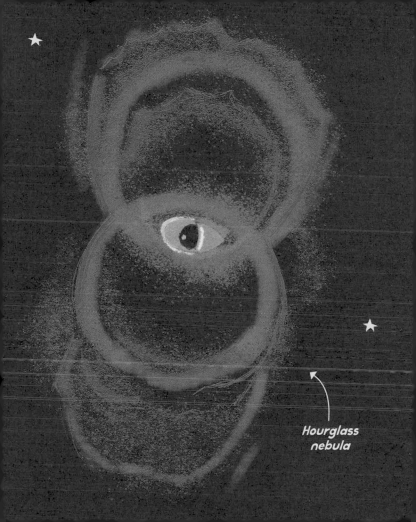

Hourglass nebula

~

By **500** BCE people knew that curved pieces of glasses, or lenses, can make things look closer. About 2,000 years later, someone put two of them together to make the first

TELESCOPE.

The year after that, in 1609, **GALILEO** used a telescope to discover new worlds, new stars, and new details on the Moon.

Galileo

You can see about **3,000 STARS** on a really dark night. The best telescopes can see around **100 TRILLION** (100 million million).

27

The mountain
MAUNA KEA
in Hawaii, USA, is one
of the least cloudy
spots on Earth, so
13 TELESCOPES
have been built there.

Many of the world's best telescopes aren't on Earth at all—they are in orbit around it. There are no clouds there to spoil the view. The best space pictures come from a space telescope called

HUBBLE.

Solar System

Venus

Mars

Mercury

Earth

Sun

The **SOLAR SYSTEM** is the Sun, Earth, Moon, and other **PLANETS** and **MOONS**. The planet closest to the Sun is Mercury, and then there are Venus, Earth, Mars, Jupiter, Saturn, Uranus, and Neptune.

Jupiter

The planets are named
after ancient gods.
MERCURY, the fastest-moving planet,
is named after the speedy messenger
god. Bright shiny VENUS is named
after the goddess of love.
Sea-blue NEPTUNE is the name
of an ocean god, and blood-colored
MARS is god of war.

Uranus

Neptune

Saturn

William Herschel

Although there are eight planets, people only knew about six of them until **1781**, when **ASTRONOMER** William Herschel spotted another one through his homemade telescope. The planet is now called **URANUS**.

William's sister Caroline was an astronomer too. She loved comets, and found lots of new ones.

34

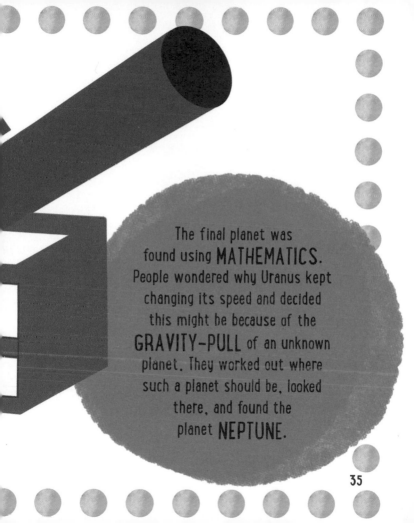

The final planet was found using **MATHEMATICS**. People wondered why Uranus kept changing its speed and decided this might be because of the **GRAVITY-PULL** of an unknown planet. They worked out where such a planet should be, looked there, and found the planet **NEPTUNE**.

The **MOON** isn't a planet: it goes around the **EARTH** rather than the **SUN**. Most of the other planets have moons too.

Every year, the Moon gets about 1.5 IN. farther from the Earth, and moves around the Earth a little more SLOWLY.

Long ago, when the
SOLAR SYSTEM
was new, there were probably
dozens of planets. Some of them
crashed together to form
the eight we know today.

Several moons in the Solar System have ICY CRUSTS with huge underground OCEANS beneath them. If there are

LIVING THINGS

elsewhere in the Solar System, they may be swimming through these oceans.

AT NIGHT ON

MERCURY,

THE PLANET CLOSEST TO
OUR SUN, THE TEMPERATURE
IS COLDER THAN A FREEZER.
ALMOST AS SOON AS THE
SUN RISES, IT SHOOTS UP
TO HOTTER THAN AN OVEN,
HOT ENOUGHT TO MELT THE
METALS LEAD AND TIN.

It can be so cold
and so hot because
MERCURY
does not have a nice thick
atmosphere to spread
the heat around.

For THOUSANDS of years, ancient people watched and even WORSHIPPED the big bright star seen just after sunset and the big bright star seen just before dawn. But until about 350 BCE no one realized that they are both

VENUS,

the second planet from the Sun.

Venus has such thick **CLOUDS** that its surface is always hidden.

The clouds are made of
SULFURIC ACID
(a liquid which dissolves metals),
the surface is oven-hot, and
there are probably endless
LIGHTNING storms too.

Every so often, huge ROCKS from space
CRASH onto the Earth. They are called

METEORITES.

As they fall, they make huge BRIGHT STREAKS
in the sky, called fireballs. The biggest
meteorite found so far weighs more
than 60 TONS (or 10 elephants).

THAT'S QUITE **TEENY**
COMPARED TO ONE THAT **BASHED**
INTO OUR PLANET MILLIONS OF
YEARS AGO. IT THREW UP SO MUCH
DUST THE SUN'S LIGHT WAS CUT
OFF, THE WORLD **FROZE**, AND
THE DINOSAURS DIED OUT.

On the
MOON
you could jump six
times higher than on EARTH.

That's because GRAVITY,
which PULLS you down
to the ground, is much
weaker there.

There's **NO AIR** on the Moon.
This means there's **NO WIND OR
RAIN**, the **SKY** is **BLACK** all day,
and the stars can be seen **ALL DAY**.

MARS IS SLIGHTLY RED BECAUSE
IT HAS GONE RUSTY. IRON IN THE
SOIL THERE HAS JOINED WITH
OXYGEN TO FORM RUST.

MARS

has weather a bit like
Earth's: sometimes there is
frost or snow, or dust storms.
Dust storms on Mars can
cover the whole planet
for months.

Between Mars and Jupiter
are lots of giant rocks
called ASTEROIDS.
The first asteroid, called
Ceres, was found in 1801,
but at first it was
called a planet.

There are
asteroids called
JAMES BOND, MR. SPOCK,
and **JABBERWOCK.**

It's always stormy on

JUPITER,

the fifth planet from the Sun.
One of these storms is so big
that it can be seen from Earth
with a telescope—people have
been watching the
red swirling storm
for over 300 years.

storm on
Jupiter

JUPITER

is such a big planet
that it weighs more than all
the others added together.

If you spin around fast enough,
your arms will naturally lift up.
A similar effect to this means that
Jupiter, which spins very fast,
bulges sideways and is shaped
like a grapefruit.

SATURN,

THE SIXTH PLANET FROM THE SUN,
HAS ENORMOUS RINGS. THEY
CONTAIN BRIGHT SHINY ICE,
MAKING THEM EASY TO SEE.
THE PLANET IS SO LIGHT
IT WOULD FLOAT IN A BOWL
OF WATER (IF THERE WAS
A BOWL OF WATER
BIG ENOUGH)!

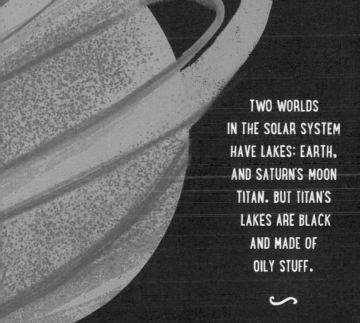

TWO WORLDS
IN THE SOLAR SYSTEM
HAVE LAKES: EARTH,
AND SATURN'S MOON
TITAN. BUT TITAN'S
LAKES ARE BLACK
AND MADE OF
OILY STUFF.

PLANETS SPIN AROUND AND SPIN AROUND AT THE SAME TIME. THEY MOVE FROM PLACE TO PLACE (AROUND THE SUN) AND SPIN AROUND AT THE SAME TIME. THEY MOVE FROM PLACE TO PLACE (AROUND THE SUN) ARE LIKE TOPS OR SPINNING COINS.

URANUS, the seventh planet, is different: it spins on its SIDE. Probably, another world CRASHED into it long ago.

If you were
born on the planet

NEPTUNE,

you would never reach
your first birthday!
Years there are 165
Earth-years long,
because it takes
Neptune that long
to go around
the Sun.

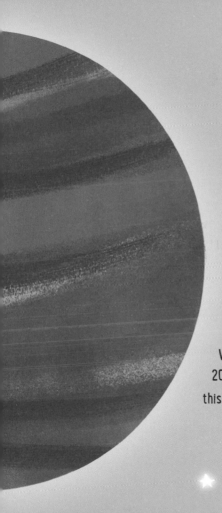

The STRONGEST
WINDS on Earth blow
at about **60 MPH.**
Winds on Neptune blow
20 times faster than
this—**ALL DAY LONG.**

59

PLUTO

USED TO BE THE NINTH PLANET FROM THE SUN,

BUT IN 2006, **ASTRONOMERS** DECIDED

IT IS TOO TEENY TO BE CALLED A PLANET

AND NOW IT IS CALLED A

DWARF PLANET

INSTEAD.

SOME OF THE MOUNTAINS,
CRATERS, AND OTHER
FEATURES ON **PLUTO**
ARE NAMED AFTER PEOPLE
AND THINGS FROM
STAR TREK, DR. WHO,
AND MONSTERS FROM
HORROR STORIES.

Beyond the planets lie millions of tiny worlds which together form the **KUIPER BELT**. These worlds are called KBOs, short for **KUIPER BELT OBJECTS**.

One **KBO** is nicknamed **SANTA**. It's covered in ice and has two tiny moons called **RUDOLPH** and **BLITZEN**, after the reindeer in the famous poem, "The Night Before Christmas."

Beyond the planets
and the Kuiper Belt
there is a huge area called
the Oort Cloud, full of
millions of icy objects like
space icebergs.

Sometimes,
objects in the **KUIPER BELT**
or the Oort Cloud start moving toward
the Sun. As they heat up they **STEAM**
and **BUBBLE**, leaving long tails of
dust and **GAS** behind them. We can
sometimes see them in the
night sky, and we call
them **COMETS**.

In 1994,
a comet broke into
pieces and fell onto
JUPITER, pulled down
by the strong **GRAVITY**
of the giant planet.

66

Stars

Next time you are on a beach, try
counting the grains in a tiny pinch
of sand. There are MORE STARS in
the SKY than there are GRAINS of
SAND on all the world's beaches.

Most STARS are twins:
PAIRS of stars which go around
each other. But they are so close
that we see each pair as a
single POINT of LIGHT.

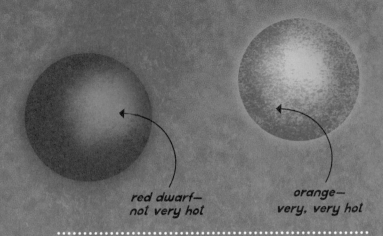

red dwarf—
not very hot

orange—
very, very hot

Most of the stars in the Universe are
small, dim, and not very hot. They are called

RED DWARFS.

Even though there are so many red dwarfs, not
a single one can be seen with the naked eye.

Red stars are usually a lot cooler than those of other colors—but still **HOTTER** than an oven. These colors are the ones the stars have when seen through a telescope.

white—spectacularly hot

yellow—ridiculously hot

blue-white—what a scorcher!

Some **STARS** grow and
shrink every few days,
weeks, or months—almost
as if they are breathing.
They are called variable
stars. Two of the oldest ones
have names meaning
"the **WONDERFUL**"
and "the **GHOUL**."

There are **STARS** that have discs around them, which are usually dusty and gassy, but some of these discs are full of **SNOW**.

A lot of
the MATERIALS you
are made from come from a
giant STAR, which EXPLODED
long ago, drifted across space,
and became part of a
SPACE CLOUD.

Eventually,
some bits of the
CLOUD
turned into our
SOLAR SYSTEM—
and, eventually,
YOU.

EXOPLANETS
are planets that go
around other stars
instead of our Sun.
An exoplanet called
TrEs-2b is completely
black. Another,
called GJ 504b, is
bright pink, and
GJ 1214b is completely
covered by an ocean.

55 Cancri E might be made
mainly of diamonds,
while Hd 189733b is
so windy that the rain
falls sideways. And the
rain there is made of glass!

GJ 1214b in front
of its parent
star

55 Cancri E

GJ 504b

Our **SUN** is
so big that about 1.3 million
Earth-sized planets could be
squeezed into it. But there are
much bigger stars: some are so
big that over a **THOUSAND
MILLION** Suns could fit
inside them. If our Sun was
that big, it would cover
the whole sky.

The Sun
is about halfway
through its life. In around
5,000 MILLION YEARS
it will get brighter, bigger, hotter,
and redder and turn into a
RED GIANT star. Mercury,
Venus, and maybe Earth will
fall into the Sun as it swells
into a red giant.

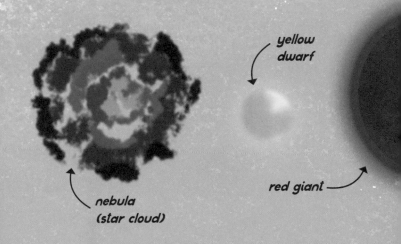

yellow
dwarf

nebula
(star cloud)

red giant

RED GIANTS keep getting bigger until they
have become huge expanding **BUBBLES** of gas
and dust called **PLANETARY NEBULAS.**
The "planetary" part of the name
is because they are usually round, like planets.

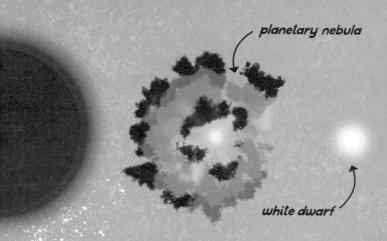

planetary nebula

white dwarf

AFTER MASSIVE
STARS
DIE, THEY OFTEN LEAVE BEHIND
TINY SHRUNKEN LEFTOVERS CALLED
WHITE DWARFS.
A TEASPOON OF THE WEIRD METAL
WHITE DWARFS ARE MADE OF WOULD
WEIGH MORE THAN A HOUSE.

Once a
WHITE DWARF
has cooled enough to become
dark, it will be a **BLACK DWARF**.
But this **COOLING** takes so long
that not a single black
dwarf exists yet.

Some stars leave behind
objects which are even more
shrunken than white dwarfs, called
NEUTRON STARS or **PULSARS**. Many
of these spin very quickly. They are a bit
like the **SPINNING LIGHTS** on police
cars, but instead of light they
send out beams of
radio signals.

IN 1957, WHEN THE SIGNALS FROM A PULSAR WERE PICKED UP ON EARTH FOR THE FIRST TIME, SOME PEOPLE THOUGHT THEY WERE MESSAGES FROM ALIENS, AND THEY WERE LABELED LGM FOR

LITTLE GREEN MEN.

In 1974, a giant **RADIO TELESCOPE** in Arecibo, Puerto Rico, sent a radio message to aliens in the form of a cartoon. So far there has been no reply.

BLACK HOLES

have gravity so strong that even light can't escape. If you got close to a black hole, the gigantic gravity would pull you out into a long, thin strand. Scientists call this **SPAGHETTIFICATION.**

When the most massive stars die, they explode.

The explosions, called **SUPERNOVAS**, are brighter than whole **GALAXIES**.

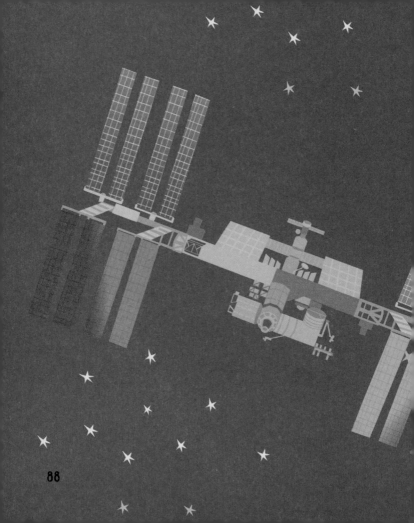

Space Travel

People have been
sending objects
that circle, or orbit,
the Earth since the
1950s. These objects are
called **SATELLITES**.
The first, Sputnik 1, was
launched from the Soviet Union
in 1957 (Russia and other countries
were part of the Soviet Union
then). It sent out radio signals
that could be heard all over
the Earth.

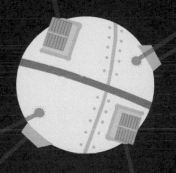

One of the first US satellites, called **VANGUARD 1**, is still in orbit today.

DRAGON SPACECRAFT are designed to take people to space stations.

There are plans to put a hotel in orbit
and take tourists to it in Dragons.

Dragons have special rockets to whisk
them swiftly away from danger.

*Dragon
Spacecraft*

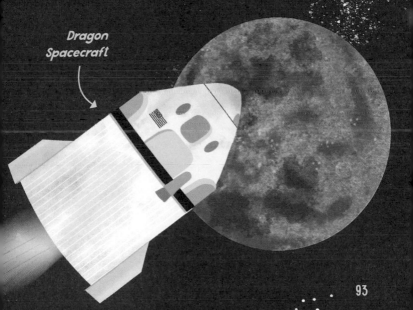

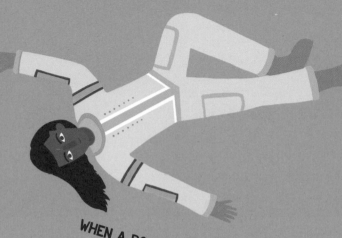

WHEN A ROCKET BLASTS OFF, IT GAINS SPEED SO FAST THAT THE ASTRONAUTS FEEL UP TO SIX TIMES HEAVIER THAN ON EARTH. BUT WHEN THE ENGINES SWITCH OFF, THEY HAVE NO WEIGHT AT ALL.

ROCKETS USE ALMOST **ALL** THEIR FUEL TO REACH SPACE. ONCE THERE, THEY **SWITCH OFF** THEIR ENGINES AND "**COAST**" FOR THOUSANDS OR EVEN MILLIONS OF MILES.

The first
FILM about an
imaginary Moon
trip was made in 1902.
The **ASTRONAUTS**
were shot to the Moon
by a **CANNON**.

Plants have been grown in space, and many ANIMALS have traveled into space, including TORTOISES, JELLYFISH, MONKEYS, SPIDERS, DOGS, and CATS.

The word astronaut means **"STAR SAILOR"**, even though astronauts don't go to the stars, nor sail anywhere.

Yuri Gagarin

The first human space
traveler was Russian-born
YURI GAGARIN,
who traveled around the
Earth in 1961, in a spacecraft
called (in Russian)
SWALLOW.
It was very cramped, and
Yuri was chosen partly
because he was small
enough to fit inside.

In 1961, US President Kennedy decided that Americans would be going to the Moon by 1970. This started a

RACE

with the Soviet Union to get there first.

Saturn V taking off

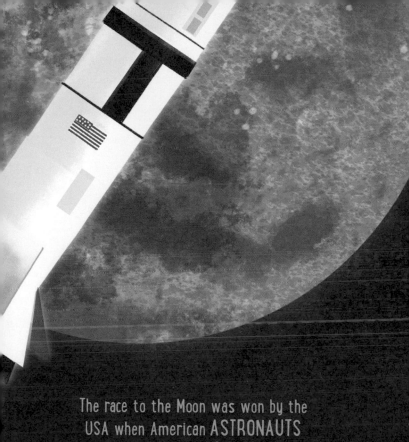

The race to the Moon was won by the
USA when American ASTRONAUTS
landed on the MOON in 1969.

A lot of **FUEL** is needed for a Moon rocket. Each Apollo rocket (called a **SATURN V**) carried 200,000 gallons of fuel, enough to fuel **10,000 CARS**. Most of this fuel was burned up in under **3 MINUTES**.

02:41

When the first **ASTRONAUTS** returned from the Moon, they went on a world tour. But first they were put in quarantine for 21 days, just in case they were carrying **MOON-GERMS**.

the crew of Apollo 11 ⟶

104

In 1971, hundreds of **TREE SEEDS** were taken
to the **MOON** and back, and later planted
on Earth, to see if they would grow into
anything **WEIRD**. Since then, the locations
of almost all have been forgotten—they've probably
grown to be just the same as normal trees.
But you never know . . .

SIX APOLLO SPACECRAFT TOOK 12 PEOPLE TO THE MOON

between 1969 and 1972. They left many things behind, including three electric cars and two golf balls.

The **APOLLO** missions that landed on the Moon were numbers 11, 12, 14, 15, 16, and 17. Why no number 13? Because part of it **BLEW UP** on the way to the Moon, so the astronauts had to repair their spaceship and go home.

MOST SPACESUITS
HAVE 16 LAYERS, AND
TAKE NEARLY AN
HOUR TO PUT ON.
THE INNER LAYER
HAS TUBES
RUNNING THROUGH IT,
WHICH CARRY COOL
WATER SO THAT
THE ASTRONAUT
DOESN'T GET
TOO HOT.

A single **SPACE SUIT** costs about **$14 MILLION.** But without one, an astronaut outside a spacecraft would die a **HORRIBLE** death!

The **WEIGHTLESS** conditions on space journeys do strange things to space **TRAVELERS:** their bones and **MUSCLES SHRINK** and weaken, and they get about an inch **TALLER.** They go back to normal when they get home.

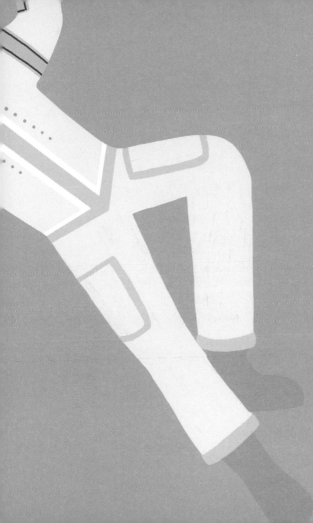

In 2018, rocket-builder **ELON MUSK** sent a car into space.

It is still **IN ORBIT** around the **SUN**.

Tortoises, bears, squirrels, and many other animals **SLEEP** for weeks or months. They do this to get through winter, when food is scarce. **SCIENTISTS** are studying ways for people to do this too, so they can make long **SPACE JOURNEYS** to distant planets.

Although **PEOPLE** have only so far reached the Moon, **ROBOT EXPLORERS** have done much better. They have **EXPLORED** every planet in the **SOLAR SYSTEM** and have landed on **MOONS, COMETS,** and **ASTEROIDS** too.

One of the fastest human-made things is the **VOYAGER 1** space probe, launched in 1977 to **EXPLORE** other planets. It's going 100 times faster than a racecar. Even at that speed, Voyager 1 won't get to a star for over **50,000** years.

Most missions
to **MARS** have failed,
with the spacecraft
CRASHING or getting **LOST**.
Scientists joke that they
are being **EATEN** by a
great galactic ghoul.

The first two probes to
land on Mars were called

VIKINGS.

In 1976 they tested the soil on
Mars for life, but the results were so
odd that even now it's not clear
what they found there.

A satellite with people
on board is called a
SPACE STATION.
The first American space station
was called SkyLab. It was launched
in 1972 and was made from a huge
fuel tank originally designed for a
Moon mission that never happened.

In 1979, after six years in space and once all the astronauts had left, **SKYLAB** crashed back to Earth—mostly onto Australia.

There have been people
LIVING in **SPACE**
every day since
November 2, 2000,
when the first three crew
members arrived at the
**INTERNATIONAL
SPACE STATION (ISS).**
The ISS was built in
sections, and is still
UNFINISHED.

Burping happens when gas, which is light, **BUBBLES** upward through the mush inside your stomach, which is heavier. But in orbit (such as in the International Space Station), nothing has weight, so there's no bubbling-up of **GAS**, and **NO ONE BURPS**.

Everything **FLOATS** on a space station,

so toilets are like **VACUUM CLEANERS**,

and suck away astronauts' **POOP** and **PEE**.

On the ISS, astronauts sleep on the walls—

their sleeping bags are **STUCK IN PLACE**

so they don't drift around.

The
Universe
and its
Galaxies

OUR SUN is one of a group of millions of stars called a galaxy. Our galaxy is called the **MILKY WAY**, and is one of many millions of galaxies, stretching out through space.

The word **GALAXY** comes from the Greek word for milk, because the Milky Way looks like someone has spilled milk across the night sky.

The **UNIVERSE** is the name given to all the **GALAXIES,** and everything else, too. Most of the stuff in the Universe is invisible. It is called **DARK MATTER.** No one knows what it is made of.

The **MILKY WAY** is a spiral galaxy. There are lots of other spiral galaxies, and many other shapes too.

The
SOMBRERO GALAXY
looks like a hat, with
a brim made of dust.
(A sombrero is a hat
with a wide brim.)

People who **STUDY** the **UNIVERSE** aren't called universologists – they're called **COSMOLOGISTS,** because "cosmos" is another word for Universe.

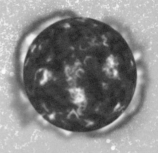

Most space objects are very old. The **EARTH, SUN,** and **MOON** are more than

4,000 MILLION

years old, and the whole Universe is about three times older than that.

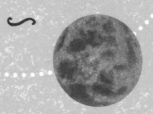

One day,
the **MILKY WAY**
will collide with another galaxy,
called **ANDROMEDA**. But,
because stars are so far apart,
very few will actually
CRASH into each other.

There is
a lot of **DUST**
in space. On a very
dark night you might see
that the Milky Way has dark
STRIPES running along it.
These are made of **CLOUDS**
of dust, getting in
the way of stars
behind them.

Most galaxies,
including ours, have
BLACK HOLES
in the middle, often millions
of times more massive
than the Sun.

They are called

SUPERMASSIVE

BLACK HOLES.

The **MICE** are a pair of galaxies that **COLLIDED** long ago. They are now moving apart again, but a long **MOUSE-TAIL** of **STARS** still connects them.

A **GALAXY**
called the Tadpole
also has a long
STAR-TAIL. 137

The **UNIVERSE**
began nearly 14 billion
(that's 14 thousand million)
years ago, in a sudden burst
of energy called the

BIG BANG.

The brightest things in the Universe are **QUASARS.** They are huge flares of **LIGHT** from things falling into black holes in distant galaxies.

〜

One **QUASAR** is surrounded by a **CLOUD.** Like clouds on Earth, it is mostly made of **WATER**—about 100 billion times as much as in our oceans.

The
UNIVERSE
is bigger today
than it was yesterday,
and will be even
BIGGER
tomorrow.

Ever since the
BIG BANG,
the Universe has
been **GROWING.**

No one knows
if or when this

**EXPANSION OF
THE UNIVERSE,**

as it is called,
will stop.

COSMOLOGISTS
have different ideas about
how the **UNIVERSE** will
end in the very far
distant **FUTURE.**

And
maybe then
it will start all
over again . . .

Some think that it will freeze,
others that it will tear itself
to pieces, and a few
that it will all crunch
up together.